Write Now!

INSIGHTS INTO CREATIVE WRITING

Write Now!

INSIGHTS INTO CREATIVE WRITING

by Anne Wescott Dodd

General Editor—Lynne Glasner

Learning Trends
a division of Globe Book Company, Inc.
New York Chicago Cleveland

Second Edition 1978.
Copyright © 1973, Learning Trends, a Division of Globe Book Company, Inc.
50 West 23rd Street, New York, N.Y. 10010

Published simultaneously in Canada by Globe/Modern Curriculum Press

ISBN: 0-87065-916-2

PHOTOGRAPHS:
NATIONAL AUDUBON SOCIETY: 37
UNITED NATIONS: 78
GEOFFREY GOVE: all other photos

DRAWINGS:
JOHN KILLIGREW

PAINTING:
ANN MEZEY: 102

PRINTED IN THE UNITED STATES OF AMERICA   12 13 14

Author

Anne Wescott Dodd has taught English and social studies in both Maine and California. She received her B.A. in social studies at the University of Maine at Orono and holds an M.A. in English from the California State College at Los Angeles.

A creative and critical writer, Mrs. Dodd has published articles in numerous periodicals; her poetry has appeared in *English Journal*.

General Editor

Lynne Glasner holds an M.A. in education from New York University and has taught in the New York public school system. She has worked as an editor for several major publishers and is currently pursuing independent publishing projects.

Acknowledgments

We wish to thank the following students for permission to use their material:

Marjorie Lewis for "Home" and "Enemies"
Jean McCurdy for "Crackers"
Sonia Rackliff for "The Darkness"
William Repetto for "The Bell"
Mindy Rosenthal for "February," "Morning," and "Happiness"
Peter Fraser Shaw for "Finally Catching On"
Eric Snowdeal, Jr. for "Victory"
Betsy Thurston for "Thunderstorm"

TABLE OF CONTENTS

About This Book

Here is a book to help you enjoy yourself through expressing your creative abilities in writing.

This book is not about correctness. It is not so much about being right as it is about being yourself. Relax. Let the exercises help you to put part of yourself down on paper. You'll learn something about writing creatively. More importantly, you'll learn about yourself and others as you put yourself in closer touch with your own feelings.

So much for what the book is not about. What is it about?

There are nine sections. The first section is called "From Abstract to Concrete." It contains a series of brief exercises. In each exercise an abstract sentence is left incomplete. You are asked to finish the sentence. You do this by using concrete words or phrases. This gives you practice in writing in detail.

Section Two is called "Expanding Your Creativity." There are four exercises. Each one gives you further practice. You can expand your concepts of ordinary, everyday objects or qualities. You can express yourself in an original way.

Section Three is titled "Some Technical Tools." Here you can learn some ways to make your writing more your own. Everyone likes to know what words to choose and what images to use. Practice on these two skills comes here.

There are five senses: sight, sound, touch, taste, and smell. How to appeal to your reader's five senses is discussed in Section Four, "Description." A good writer should be able to appeal to one sense in particular. He should also be able to bring in several senses when he writes.

In Section Five, you try "Exploring the Short Story." You can get experience here in treating plot, character, setting, and dialogue. Here also is a chance to try writing a short story.

Section Six ("Exploring Drama") does the same thing for drama. First you study the special parts of drama. Then you try your hand.

"Exploring Poetry" is Section Seven. Here you study the

x

sounds of poetry. Then you write some poems. If you like to express and convey your feelings, this is the place to try.

Some brief but enjoyable creative activities are in Section Eight. Section Nine simply lists some reminders that are helpful in writing more effectively.

Besides the nine sections, directions are given on keeping a journal. You are told how to complete a term project. The book also includes an agreement or contract between you and your teacher. This contract concerns your grade.

There you have an aerial photo of the book. We believe in this book. We really think you will like it too.

Journal

Keep a journal while you are taking this course. In it you can express your thoughts and feelings—anything, in fact, that is meaningful to you. You may wish to write stories or poems. You may prefer to write personal experiences.

Write something each day. Although entries will vary in length, each one should represent at least ten minutes of writing time. Be sure to date your entries.

Your teacher will want to look at your journal regularly. It is unwise, however, to write your journal to please the teacher. Keep your journal to please yourself. Do not worry unnecessarily about spelling, grammar, and neatness. There are only two important rules for your journal.

1. You must date each entry and keep the entries in order in a notebook or folder.
2. You must write something every day. Set a goal for yourself. Write a certain number of minutes a day.

Term Project

In most courses a term project is a major part of your work. In this course your term project is a chance to be you.

Begin thinking early about what you are going to do. Feel free to use any idea of your own, remembering that your teacher may want to discuss it with you. Some suggestions are listed below.

1. Write a short story (in addition to the one assigned in Section Five). It should be at least five pages long.
2. Write a number of poems and collect them into a small book or pamphlet.
3. Write a children's book.
4. Write a short novel.
5. Write a number of poems and make them into posters.
6. Write a one-act play.

There are certainly other possibilities. You may wish to discuss illustrations, for example, with your teacher. The important thing to remember is that your term project is a major part of your work for this course. So make certain that you and your teacher agree on it.

Suggested Contract

A course in creative writing may present special problems in grading. Therefore, some teachers and students think a special agreement about grades in creative writing is needed. The following outline (or some variation of it) is presented as a suggestion. It may or may not be helpful in your situation. Again, make certain that you and your teacher both understand the basis on which you will be given a grade.

In order to receive a grade of "C," you must:

1. Keep a journal daily.
2. Complete all other assignments on time. (Make arrangements with your teacher for making up work missed because of absence.)
3. Participate in a positive manner on a regular basis in class discussions.
4. Complete a term project.

In order to receive a grade of "B," you must:

1. Complete all of the requirements for a grade of "C."
2. Submit a second term project.

In order to receive a grade of "A," you must:

1. Complete all of the requirements for a grade of "C."
2. Submit both a second term project and additional work designated by the teacher.

Of course, all of your work is evaluated and graded by your teacher. In some instances, students have signed contracts indicating their intentions to work for certain grades. If you and your teacher agree, you can copy the following form on a sheet of paper, fill it out, and give it to your teacher. Do not write in this book.

I, _____, contract for a grade of_____ in Creative Writing.

Date _____   Signed _____

Write Now!

INSIGHTS INTO CREATIVE WRITING

SECTION ONE:

From Abstract to Concrete

This section contains a group of short exercises to give you practice in using *abstract* and *concrete* words.

Abstract words are words for qualities, feelings, or ideas. They are words that tell about concepts you can't touch, or taste, or smell, or hear, or see. They are words like *happiness, anger, sadness,* or *humor.* Concrete words are different. They are words that stand for things that you can see, hear, touch, smell, or taste— words like *clown, spinach, raindrops, drums, chewing gum,* and *maple trees.*

In each of the following exercises an abstract sentence is left unfinished. In your notebook, finish each sentence using concrete words or phrases. Each unfinished sentence should call to mind many different ideas or images.

Read the examples. These have been given to suggest the kind of concrete ideas or images to look for. These examples were not written by famous writers, but by teachers, editors, and students like you.

For each sentence write at least ten words, or a number of phrases, which you think complete it well. Think of as many different images as you can. Try to find words and phrases that will let someone else see what you see, or will help someone remember something pleasant or unpleasant.

1

Use words and phrases that say exactly what you mean. Detailed and concrete words and phrases make the most exciting and successful images.

Feel free to tell your real thoughts in a concrete way. Remember that there is no limit to your ideas. They cannot be placed in a right or a wrong list.

You may complete these exercises in any order that you wish. Later, you may wish to come back to them and rework some of your ideas. You may even wish to write a paragraph or short story using some of your work. Perhaps this section will be helpful to you when you come to the other sections.

In general, you will find that the images you like best are the most concrete ones—the ones that remind you of real people, things, or happenings. These are the hardest to write, but they will also be the most satisfying and pleasing to you.

Freedom is . . . . . .
sandals and dungarees
a black president
an open door
Mr. and Ms.
marching for a cause

Love is . . . . . .
a song that means something special to you
smiling eyes
walking the dog
one red rose
a park bench

Loneliness is . . . . . .
moving away
Sunday
imprisonment
an empty mailbox
an abandoned building

Happiness is . . . . . .
the last day of school
sleeping late
a pajama party
making the team
a seat on a crowded bus or train

Wonder is . . . . . .
an astronaut
a skyscraper
the Beatles
a Rolls Royce
a rainbow

Beauty is . . . . . .
a clear running brook
the city at night
store windows at Christmas
new shoes
a clean street

Peace is . . . . . .
a moonlit meadow
soft snow
private places
accepting an apology
a sleeping block

Winter is . . . . . .
ice-shagged branches
a slumbering bear
cold fingers and toes
soggy mittens and wet boots
wind coming through the windows

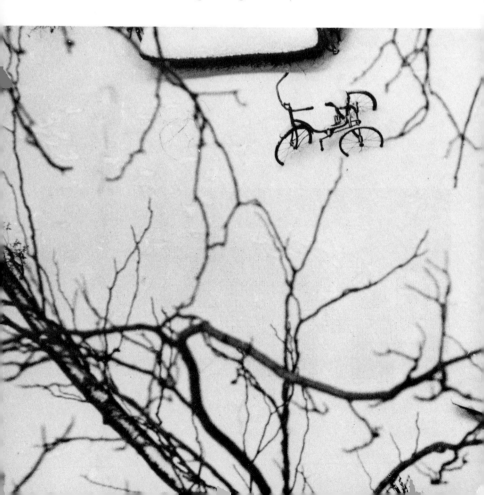

War is . . . . . .
tanks and trenches
mud
the whine of jet engines
a brother who never came home
waiting for letters

Death is . . . . . .
a slow-moving hearse
a wailing siren
an empty room
a syringe
silence

Hate is . . . .
a rat
an overturned garbage can
a locked door
being kept inside
a whining sister

Sadness is . . . . . .
your best friend moving away
a wilted flower
deep blue
a broken window
one parent

Spring is . . . . . .
kites and bikes
warm breezes
balloons and hot dogs
sweaters
rain on the roof

Kindness is . . . . . .
warmth
an outstretched hand
a smiling welcome
waving to the new kid next door
change for the soda machine

Autumn is . . . . . .
apples and chestnuts
a new notebook
Saturday afternoons
the smell of burning leaves
a beginning

Anger is . . . . . .
the edge of explosion
slammed doors
fists
a broken promise
an engine starting

Fear is . . . . . .
the unknown
roller coasters
not asking a question
a doctor's waiting room
an absent parent

Wisdom is . . . . . .
planting trees
making a mistake once
a discovery
a parent who knows the right thing to say
an extra blanket on an overnight hike

Summer is . . . . . .
seaweed and seashells
watermelon
a crowded stoop
an open fire hydrant
a melting ice cream cone

SECTION TWO:

Expanding your Creativity

Accurate and original descriptions are basic to creative writing. The more you think about an object, scene, or situation, the more aspects of it you can describe. The exercises in this section are intended to give you practice in expanding your concepts of ordinary, familiar things and expressing them in a fresh, unspoiled way.

You should complete this section before going on to the sections that follow. Try to do these exercises in the order in which they appear. If you do get stuck, go on to the next exercise, and then return to the incomplete one.

As an additional tip, it will probably help you to write down *all* of your thoughts. After you have done this, you can choose the better ones from what you have written. Bear in mind that originality in expression is really what turns something apparently dull or uninteresting into something new, exciting, and creative.

Answerless Questions

Answer each question. Give a reason for your answer.
Example: What color is surprise? Yellow,
because it happens so suddenly.

1. Which is colder, an iceberg or fear?
2. Which is itchier, a wool sweater or curiosity?
3. Which is softer, a kiss or cotton?
4. What shape is life?
5. What color is noise?
6. Which is warmer, love or the sun?
7. Which is more sour, a lemon or defeat?
8. Which is happier, sunrise or sunset?
9. What color is winning?
10. Which is slower, K or Z?

Now make up ten questions like the ones above. If it is possible to do so, ask one of your classmates to answer your questions. At the same time you can be working on your classmate's questions.

Brainstorming

"Brainstorming" is a method used to get ideas. The more ideas you have, the better the chances of getting good ones. Brainstorming means listing on paper every thought you have about a subject. This may be done alone or, with permission, in small groups. The purpose is to come up with as many ideas as possible. Quantity, not quality, is the first consideration.

Brainstorming may help you choose a better plot for a story or write a more unusual poem. Don't ever stop with your first idea, although that may be the idea you end up using. Brainstorm all the possibilities; then choose the best.

A. Brainstorming by yourself. Think of as many uses as you can for the following items. See how original you can be.
1. a paper clip
2. a potato
3. a book
4. a door
5. a blank sheet of paper
6. a button
7. a shoelace
8. an empty soda can
9. a paper cup
10. a toothpick
B. Brainstorming with others. With your teacher's permission, form small groups. In your group, brainstorm uses for a cement block with your classmates. Again, list all ideas, even the most ridiculous. Don't spend time discussing any of them. When the teacher tells you that your time is up, choose someone to report your group's list to the rest of the class.

Color Associations

What colors do you see when you think of each of the following? Why?

Each day of the week

Your school

Your family

Your best friend

Now reverse your thinking. What do the following colors make you think of? Perhaps some of the colors will remind you of abstract ideas such as happiness or sadness. Perhaps others will remind you of concrete objects. Make your ideas original. Nearly everyone associates red with danger, and it is really rather easy to say that yellow makes one think of a canary.

List at least four really fresh ideas for each color.

red

blue

yellow

green

white

black

brown

orange

pink

Word Combinations

The meaningful combination of words is what makes writing sensible, interesting, and often creative. You may be surprised at the different combinations of words you can write by starting with only three words and adding other words to make a meaningful sentence.

Write a sentence using all the words listed after each number in the following exercise. The sentences may be long or short, but they must make sense. Try to make them clever by using the words in a slightly different manner. Don't settle for your first combination. Shift the words around. Substitute. Improvise. Try every possibility. Then choose the best.

Example: puddle   step   ginger

You might write, "The ginger-haired dog stepped in the puddle." A more unusual sentence would be, "Ginger learned the new puddle dance step." Maybe you would like to "invent" a new product. For example, "Ginger Steps, the new waterproof shoes, don't mind going in puddles." Notice that some words can be used as more than one part of speech.

1.	whistle	hair	bubble gum
2.	train	elevator	sirens
3.	match	flash	tree
4.	stump	heel	blonde
5.	marble	candy	walk
6.	boot	bottle	run
7.	ball	surprise	jinx
8.	paper	black	cream
9.	pipe	fog	step
10.	fall	flesh	stone

SECTION THREE:

Some Technical Tools

Included here are five exercises on figures of speech and one on word choice. These six are grouped together because they all belong in a writer's toolbox. Sharp, effective writing results, in part, from using these tools well. But it takes a lot of practice to learn which tool to use as well as when and how to use it.

Follow the directions for each exercise. You will be pleased to see that they are both challenging and rewarding.

Expressed Comparison

In our everyday conversation, we often make expressed or direct comparisons between two unlike objects. We do this to clarify what we wish to explain. Normally, an expressed comparison is introduced by the words *like* or *as*.

For example, a girl may have cheeks "like roses." A clever boy may be smart "as a fox." Many of these expressions are now trite. In other words, they have been used so often that they are worn-out—no longer fresh, original, or effective.

Complete the phrases below by adding a word or words which makes an original but sensible comparison. Avoid using words you have heard before in the same phrase. Expand your thinking.

Example: busy as a mustard paddle at a
wiener roast

 1. clever as
 2. funny as
 3. happy as
 4. quick as
 5. tired as
 6. frightened as
 7. sneaky as
 8. nervous as
 9. silly as
10. thin as

An expressed or direct comparison is sometimes called a *simile* [SIM uh lee]. A simile is a literary device which helps a reader better understand what you are trying to say. Similes are used in both prose and poetry. An original simile is fun to read. A trite one is boring.

Implied Comparison

Unlike expressed comparisons, implied or indirect comparisons are not introduced by the words *like* or *as*. Implied comparisons can be made by connecting two unlike objects by their common quality. Such statements are meant comparatively, not literally. For example, "John is a clown" does not mean that John dresses in baggy pants and has his face painted. Rather, John's actions draw the laughter of other people, so he brings to mind a circus clown. Many implied comparisons are tired and worn-out through overuse. If they are not trite, however, they can be very effective.

Write an implied comparison for each of the following.

Example: Old age is a summer evening.

1. a building
2. motherhood
3. an elephant
4. authority
5. a snowflake
6. a traffic light
7. a tree
8. a graveyard
9. a subway tunnel
10. a bicycle

An implied or indirect comparison is usually called a *metaphor* [MET uh for]. Use metaphors to create poems and prose that are fresh and alive. At this point you may wish to look back at the metaphors you wrote in Section One. Can you improve any of these metaphors now?

Personification

A writer must be sensitive. He must feel with his characters. He must write so that the reader can identify with the people and places he talks about. If you can put yourself in someone else's place, you become more aware of that person's feelings. If you try to imagine what it would be like to be a particular object, such as a pencil, a coin, or a telephone, you can get new ideas on description and identification.

To give an animal or inanimate object human qualities such as thinking or feeling is called personification [pur sahn if uh KAY shun]. Many writers use this device to make their work more exciting.

Write a paragraph or poem in which you are some object or animal. What is life like for you? What makes you happy? Sad? What do you hope for?

Here is an example of personification:

Mary was just about to slam the phone down on its cradle when the telephone talked back!

"Don't do that," it pleaded, "Not again! Don't you realize that I'm a sensitive instrument? Do you think I like busy signals any more than you do? Oh, that ugly buzzing, buzzing, buzzing, it gives me a frightful receiver-ache. And instead of sympathy you crash me down on my cradle. You know, I bruise very easily. I'm a Princess Phone, and you treat me like any common kitchen wall phone: gossiping into my delicate speaker; letting my beautiful curly cord get all twisted and knotted up; dialing wrong numbers till my wires get crossed; ignoring my pretty ringing sounds. You just don't deserve me. Aren't you ashamed?"

Some suggestions follow below.

1. a television
2. a watch
3. a coin
4. a dog
5. a shoe
6. a tiger
7. a door
8. a tree
9. a porpoise
10. a garbage can

Do you think you have given a new picture of the animal or object you have chosen?

Exaggeration

Many times people exaggerate to make a point. Do you remember telling your friends that you "stayed up all night studying for the test"? Or have you heard a girl say, "When we broke up, I cried for weeks"?

Write a statement about each of the following subjects in which you exaggerate to make a point. The subject areas are broad. You may wish to narrow them down in making your statements.

Example: His heart warmed the entire world.

1. weather
2. hunger
3. a basketball game
4. an injury
5. an empty house
6. the United States
7. an animal
8. a color
9. the size or weight of something
10. a crowded train

This kind of exaggeration is a literary device called *hyperbole* [hi PUR buh lee]. It is used in both poetry and prose. Of course, these statements should not be taken literally; they are "larger than life" in order to make a point. Sometimes hyperbole is used along with a simile or metaphor to make a comparison. Example: He is as friendly as a candidate for office.

Apparent Contradiction

Here are some expressions which, at first glance, do not seem to make sense. However, if you think about them, you can imagine situations which explain them very well.

Example: sad laughter—laughing to be polite while being unhappy about something

Can you explain the following seemingly contradictory expressions? Does your explanation make sense to you?

1. warmly cold
2. screaming silence
3. slow hurrier
4. dark sunshine
5. calm terror
6. chilling warmth

Now make up ten phrases containing apparent contradictions. If possible, exchange lists with a classmate. Try to explain each other's list.

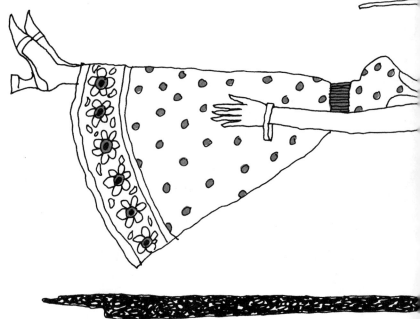

Word Choice

"Four score and seven years ago our fathers brought forth on this continent a new nation, conceived in liberty, and dedicated to the proposition that all men are created equal."

The opening sentence from Lincoln's "Gettysburgh Address" is very famous. Almost everyone admires the way it is written. Have you ever wondered how the sentence might read if Lincoln had not been such a good writer?

"Eighty-seven years ago some people started a new country, born in freedom, and based on the idea that everybody's equal."

This version is simpler but has none of Lincoln's majesty and stateliness. The idea is obvious. A writer must choose the right word for the right situation. As you gain more practice in writing, you will enjoy choosing the most fitting words.

The best time to tinker with your choice of words comes when you revise. Don't try to say something perfectly the first time you say it. Good writing includes revising. Remember also that the simplest word is often the best one. *End*, do not *terminate*, your sentences with periods.

Make a list of ten quotable statements made by authors, statesmen, or other public figures. Try to analyze why the words in each statement make it effective. It is always a good idea to write down a statement that impresses you. Believe it or not, your own writing will improve as a result of your doing so.

Like imagery, word choice is an important tool.

SECTION FOUR:

Description

This group of exercises gives you practice in writing description. To do this most effectively, you must appeal to the reader's five senses. All but one of these exercises deals with one of the five senses. In these you are asked to use descriptions which emphasize only one sense in particular, though others may be mentioned. In the last exercise ("Getting It Together") you are asked to combine all five senses in one piece of description.

You may find that you can make use of some of the material you have already written in other sections. If this is so, select only the best and then capitalize on it. Of course, you may also improve some of your past ideas to create new material for this section.

Sight

This exercise deals with your sense of sight. When a writer describes something, he must recreate a scene for the reader. Being as concrete as possible, he must describe all of those things which make the scene alive and real.

All around you are many scenes to describe. What you need to do is paint a picture with words. A description does not come alive unless you give details so that the reader can SEE the picture you have "painted." Here's a chance to use what you have learned about figures of speech in Section Three.

Think of a phrase or sentence about each object. Then describe all the details you can, so that your reader will see the object in the same way you did.

Example: automobile—a lemon yellow sports car
with sun-struck chrome that burns the eyes

1. fence
2. building
3. traffic light
4. motorcycle
5. tree
6. book
7. face
8. room
9. park
10. bus

Try your hand now at writing a complete paragraph or poem describing a scene or event. Include only those details which the reader can SEE in his mind. The topics listed below are suggestions.

1. the school playground
2. a basketball game
3. a vacant lot
4. a city street
5. a spring day
6. a river
7. a sunset
8. a bridge
9. a parade
10. an empty building

Hearing

Most of us are dependent on our sense of sight. Our other senses, including hearing, are often not as developed as they could be. Yet a writer can bring originality and freshness to his writing by appealing to other senses besides sight. Be prepared to listen better so that you can write about the way things sound.

Write a word, phrase, or sentence for each of the following. Make your reader HEAR the sound in his mind.

Example: a chair

The chair scraped and scratched its way across the floor.

1. a table
2. a movie theatre (before the movie begins)
3. a television western scene
4. school dismissal
5. a fire truck
6. dogs barking
7. rain
8. a traffic jam
9. someone preparing dinner
10. a guitar playing

A rather specialized way to put sound in writing is to use words that imitate or suggest certain sounds. Words which sound like their meaning are *onomatopoetic* [ah nuh ma tuh po ET ik].

Example: The bee *buzzed* as the *bubble* burst.

Onomatopoeia [ah nuh ma tuh PEE yuh] often perks up writing and makes it come alive for the reader.

Try writing an entire paragraph or poem describing the sounds that might be heard in a particular scene. The following list contains suggestions. Remember—sounds only.

1. the school cafeteria
2. a city street in a foreign country
3. an airplane ride
4. a train crash
5. a walk in the park
6. a moonless night in a haunted house
7. a rock 'n roll concert
8. a dripping sink
9. a crowded store
10. a fire

Touch

This exercise is similar to the ones on sight and sound. Describe the following items by using only those qualities which the reader could FEEL by touching the object. Use any literary device that will make the reader feel as if he is actually touching the object.

Write a phrase or a sentence to describe the way the following items feel when you touch them.

1. concrete
2. a snake
3. a polished wood table
4. a tree trunk
5. a melted candle
6. an old pair of dungarees
7. a glass
8. custard
9. finger paint
10. an ice cube

Now write a paragraph or poem describing an object or scene which appeals to the reader's sense of touch. Use phrases that will make the reader feel as if he is able to reach out and touch the item described. Select items that have a distinct texture and/or shape.

Below are some additional suggestions, but you may choose items from the previous list.

1. styrofoam
2. your desk at school
3. dust
4. a pen or pencil
5. a bottle
6. sand
7. a piece of metal
8. an item of clothing

Taste

Taste and smell are closely related. A creative description of how something tastes will make the reader's mouth water.

For each of the following items, write a phrase which describes how the item tastes.

1. a hot dog
2. an ice cream cone
3. a lemon
4. potato chips
5. spinach
6. pizza
7. gum
8. ketchup
9. french fried potatoes
10. chocolate

A good way to tell how well you have done is to read someone *only your description* of each of the above items. Do not mention the item. Can that person tell what you have described?

As a further exercise, try your hand at writing a restaurant menu. Include at least ten foods. Try to appeal to your potential "customer's" sense of taste.

Now write a paragraph or poem describing the taste of a particular food. Use comparisions, both implied and expressed. You can describe what you ate yesterday, your favorite food, your least favorite food, or anything else, as long as it appeals only to the reader's sense of taste.

Smell

You use your sense of smell every day to identify many items by their odors, both good and bad. A good writer can make his descriptions come alive by appealing to his reader's sense of smell.

Write a phrase or sentence for each of the following, describing how each object smells. Use the literary devices you have learned to stimulate the reader's sense of smell. Remember you are appealing *only* to the sense of smell.

1. mustard
2. a bakery
3. freshly cut grass
4. paint
5. tar
6. a gas station
7. a new car
8. wet wool
9. a fish market
10. a hospital

Write a paragraph or poem describing a scene or situation that appeals only to the reader's sense of smell. Try to capture the distinctive odor of the scene you choose to describe. Use comparisons. The following list contains some suggestions.

1. a room in your school
2. a pizzeria
3. your neighborhood
4. a lunch counter
5. a zoo
6. a movie theater
7. a crowded train
8. a doctor's office
9. a bakery
10. a florist

Getting It Together

Write a paragraph or two creating a scene. Appeal to ALL of the reader's senses—sight, sound, touch, taste, and smell—in your description. Make sure you include each sense at least once. Your reader should feel as though he's right in your setting, as he reads what you have written.

Some suggested topics follow.

1. a supermarket
2. a day at the beach or pool
3. an accident
4. eating at a restaurant
5. a day in the mountains
6. a school dance or game
7. a wedding
8. a movie theater
9. visiting a museum
10. a riot

Exploring the Short Story

Up to now you have dealt with some parts of writing. This section gives you a chance to deal with a type of literature, the short story. The exercises here are on the elements of the short story: setting, plot, character, and dialogue. After you have studied each element, you can try writing your own short story.

Setting the Scene

Both the mood and the underlying meaning of a short story can be established immediately by a story's setting. A melancholy story, for example, could begin with a gray-washed description of a town. The natural elements in the scene could be described in subdued images. Other kinds of stories would begin other ways.

What does setting include? The answer really is up to you. Setting can include many far-reaching things: weather, time, and season are good mood creators. So are concrete, specific details.

Write a paragraph describing a house for the opening scene of a mystery. Write another paragraph describing the same house as it might be seen for a comedy. Do not include people in these paragraphs, although you may show evidence of people (toys on the front lawn, music coming from an open window, etc.). Remember to appeal to your reader's five senses, to use comparisons, and to create a mood.

Plot

A good plot is essential to an effective story. In a good plot the main character is involved in a conflict which produces tension for the reader. This motivates the reader to finish the story, because he wants to know how everything turns out. In general, the main character seeks a specific goal. However, he is prevented from reaching this goal by some kind of obstacle or obstacles.

Problems arise when the main character deals with these

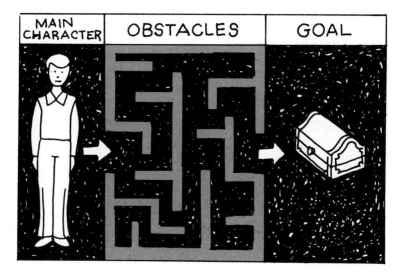

obstacles in trying to achieve this goal. Each obstacle produced is an episode in the story. The plot consists of a series of related episodes that lead to the climax. (These episodes are like scenes in a television drama.) The climax is the point at which the hero is either able to reach his goal or loses it once and for all. The conclusion quickly follows the climax.

A story may end with the hero obtaining his goal through his hard work or ingenuity. Or it may end with his being unable to reach his goal, usually because of some flaw in his character or an error in judgment. If the hero loses, he usually gains some insight from his failure. As you can see, plot is never really separate from character in a good story.

Let's look at an example.

Basic plot: John is determined to be accepted at a college for which he must have top grades and a great variety of extracurricular activities. John is not very good in math and has little time to study—so he cheats.

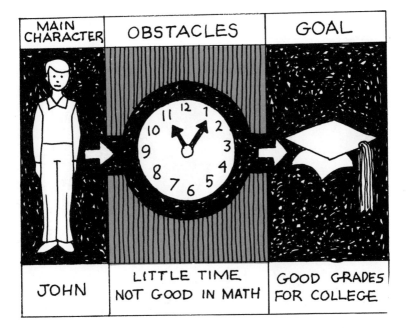

MAIN CHARACTER	OBSTACLES	GOAL
JOHN	LITTLE TIME NOT GOOD IN MATH	GOOD GRADES FOR COLLEGE

Episodes:

1. John's father insists that John get all A's and B's.
2. His mother pushes him into all kinds of activities.
3. John cheats on his math test. He's nervous, but doesn't get caught.
4. John's conscience bothers him during a National Honor Society initiation. (He's president of NHS.)
5. John cheats on a second math test but again, doesn't get caught.
6. John's girl friend talks about a boy who cheated on a French test and how she despises cheaters.
7. John takes college boards—can't cheat on these.
8. He nervously awaits scores.
9. The envelope comes back—scores are very low. John's father is angry.
10. The college turns him down. John is sadder, but perhaps wiser.

Where is the climax? Why? How is the plot tied to character?

Think of a story you could write. Use people, places, and situations with which you are familiar. The characters and situations you describe will appear most realistic if you base them upon people and events you know. Outline the plot, listing all the episodes and the ending. Indicate connections between plot and character in your outline. Identify the point at which the climax occurs.

One more point: You have heard the expression "Truth is stranger than fiction." Readers will not believe some situations in a story which occur in real life because they appear too melodramatic (like soap operas on TV—one crisis after another) or they are too far-fetched (coincidence can be overdone). The best stories and story endings are simple and believeable, or add a slightly unexpected twist. People are not likely to believe an ending in which characters live "happily ever after."

You may wish to change your outline as your thinking deepens about your plot line. There is no reason not to do this.

Character

Characterization is very important in a story. A character may be revealed in several ways:
1. his physical appearance and dress
2. what he says, thinks, feels, and dreams
3. what he does and does not do
4. what others say about him and how they react to him

A character is not usually described in a story all at one time (as you will do here). Rather, the information is given to the reader a little at a time. Sometimes, however, it may be necessary to give a short sketch of your main character at or near the beginning of the story.

How would you describe your best friend (or worst enemy)? If you wanted to give an accurate picture of someone to another person who didn't know him, you wouldn't use vague words, such as *nice, cute,* etc. A couple of anecdotes about the kinds of things a person does will reveal more about him than a long list of adjectives. Don't *tell* the reader about your characters. Let your characters *show* themselves to the reader.

Below is a sample character sketch which shows, rather than tells, the reader what kind of person Joyce is.

Joyce can always help you change your mood; if you're happy and cheerful, five minutes with her will cure that. Joyce doesn't like anything. "That English class stinks," she'll declare. "It's so-o-o boring, and that teacher gives us too much homework. She's mean!" Later, she'll tell anyone who'll listen, "Math is bad, bad, bad! I hate that class. That teacher is always picking on me."

One day in history class the teacher asked her to stop talking. She continued whispering to Janet. The teacher repeated the command in a louder voice. "I wasn't talking," Joyce shouted. "You're always leaning on me. Leave me alone!" She stormed out of the room, slamming the door behind her.

The next day the scene was repeated except that Joyce screamed, "I'm not chewing gum! Are you calling me a liar?" as she stuck some gum under the desk. When I saw Joyce later at lunch, Harriet was asking her to go to the movies. Joyce stomped her foot and growled, "No! You are going with Sue. I won't go anywhere with Sue. She's creepy! You said you'd go with me!" Like I said, Joyce can make anyone unhappy!

Now write a character sketch of someone you know. Let the reader decide from your paragraph what kind of person you are describing. Show—don't tell.

Study the pictures of these two people very carefully. Decide what kinds of people they are and what kinds of lives they lead. Keep in mind the techniques you used in writing your character sketch, and write separate sketches for each of these two individuals. Invent the examples you need to support your general statements.

Don't tell about either character. Let each character show himself. Do not attempt to combine or relate the two characters at all. These are two separate sketches.

Imagine that the young man and the old woman you have just sketched are now isolated from the rest of the world.

They are on an island or somewhere else where they are without any other human contacts. Find a reason for their isolation. Explain how they got where they now are. Keeping in mind the kind of person each one is (according to your character sketches), outline a plot or write a summary telling what happens to them. How do they get along? Do they understand each other? What kinds of problems do they have? How do they resolve them?

Dialogue

Dialogue [DIE uh log] is conversation.

Almost all short stories have at least some dialogue. Dialogue can be used:
1. to develop character
2. to keep the reader's interest
3. to advance the plot
4. to add humor
5. to make a story more realistic

Much can be revealed about people from their conversation. You can create a very humorous or tense scene just by having two people talk to each other.

Choose a scene with two characters, and have them talk. Write the conversation just as you would hear it. Remember, you must begin a new paragraph each time the speaker changes. What your characters say must appear in quotation marks.

Read the sample that follows before proceeding. It was written by a student.

Finally Catching On

"Peter, come in here for a moment. I want to speak to you," piped Mrs. White.

"Oh, oh," groaned my friend Mike, "you've been had!"

So I strolled into the lab. "Peter," squeaked Mrs. White.

"Yes," I replied.

"As I was going through the biology notes last night, I noticed that your notes and Sue's and Kevin's and Hal's and Dorothy's were pretty much indentical for experiment nine."

"Oh . . . oh, yeah?" I stuttered.

"Oh, yeah," snorted Mrs. White. "Why do five people all have identical notes for the same experiment?"

"Why?" I queried.

"Yes, why?"

"Aww," I mumbled, "no one would donate any blood so we could continue the experiment, so we all had to get our notes from Sue."

At this point Mr. Jones entered with, "Are you copying notes from each other this early in the year? You could have waited a few more weeks, couldn't you, Pete?"

"No," I replied, "we had the experiment now, not in a couple of weeks," as I slipped through the door into the comparative safety of the cafeteria.

In the dialogue above, the student wrote without using the word *said*. Some writers prefer to use a variety of words to mean *said*. There is no rule. Probably the best practice is to write the most natural way for you.

Write a sample conversation between two characters. Here are some suggested topics:

1. a woman driver explaining why she shouldn't get a ticket
2. someone returning a defective article to a department store
3. a girl telling a friend how she will explain flunking two subjects to her parents
4. a car salesman telling a woman why she needs a new car
5. a student explaining to his teacher why he wants to drop out of school
6. someone giving directions (subway, bus, train, street) to a foreigner
7. someone explaining to a store manager that he would be suited for a job as a stock clerk
8. a woman explaining how to prepare a particular recipe to someone who is learning how to cook
9. someone explaining football to another person who has never seen the game

The Short Story

You have already written several parts of a short story. Now create an original story. Write a good opening, remembering that from the first word you are creating the mood for your story. Develop your characters by showing them in action, not telling about them. Use conversation. Make sure that your plot has a conflict which can be developed to build the reader's suspense.

SECTION SIX:

Exploring Drama

Drama has much in common with fiction. However, a play is different from a short story or novel. When his play is written, the playwright expects his work to be performed by actors on a stage. A fiction writer knows his work will be read, not performed. In this section you will use what you learned in "Exploring the Short Story." But because plays are performed, there is more to learn.

Of course, there are many types of plays—some comic, some tragic—but all include certain features. Several aspects of playwriting are setting, stage direction, dialogue, scenes, and acts. Each is an important part of playwriting. Each helps actors to perform in the manner in which the author intended.

Setting and Stage Direction

Before a playwright begins the dialogue in a particular scene, he must write the setting. This describes how the stage should look. In the setting, the playwright may include information about the time, place, and people in the scene. For example, if the play opens in a living room, the playwright may state the month, year, time of day, where the living room is, and if it is large or small, richly or poorly furnished. He may go on to describe the furniture. He may name the characters in the room and describe them.

Stage direction is the method by which the playwright tells his characters where they should stand and move on stage. When we see a play, it often looks as if the actors walk freely. Actually, their movements may have been written into the play by the playwright. If there are people on stage when the scene begins, the writer gives stage directions for them.

Create settings and stage directions for the following situations or places. You may include people in your settings.

Example: Setting for a play which opens in a restaurant.

It is early evening in a dimly lit restaurant. The room has dirty white walls. At left, there are three tables covered with red-and-white checked tablecloths. At right is a counter with four stools. Dishes are piled up at the end of the counter. A ceiling fan turns slowly. A man in his early 30's sips a cup of coffee at the counter. A gray-haired waiter wearing a greasy apron stands behind the counter, holding a fly swatter.

1. a school dance
2. a street in your neighborhood
3. a block party
4. a bank robbery
5. an automobile accident
6. a living room where a boy is meeting his date's parents for the first time

Dramatic Dialogue

The bulk of the playwright's work is the creation of lively, realistic dialogue. In a short story, the author can write dialogue that ends with, "yelled Mr. Sampson, angrily." The playwright's dialogue includes only those words actually spoken by his characters. He can, however, include mood or emotion in stage directions.

The form for writing dialogue is simple. The name of the character is written in capital letters followed by a period. Directions as to how the line is spoken are put in parentheses after the name. Each time a different character speaks, his name must be written before his lines. Dialogue is not written in quotation marks.

For example, look at the following dialogue.

BOB. (Terrified, open-eyed). Wh-what are you goin' to do to me? I didn't do it. Please believe me. I DIDN'T DO IT!

JUDGE.(Coldly). Perhaps you didn't. But I can't take chances. I believe that you're a thief and a liar. And there are too many of your type loose in the streets as it is. Guards! Take him away.

BOB. (Falling to his knees). You'll be sorry, Judge. Just you wait and see. I ain't gonna forget this. You'll be sorry. . . . (He is dragged across stage and exits with the two guards.)

Write several lines of dialogue in response to each line below. Pretend you are the person to whom the statement is directed. How would you answer?

1. Father. (In surprise). Where did you get that black eye?

2. Mother.(Angrily). If you take one more step, just keep on going and don't come back.

3. Teenage girl. (Very upset). I don't ever want to see you again. How *could* you have taken Cathy to the movies last night?

4. Policeman. (Calmly). This is your last chance to come clean. Where's the money?

5. Teacher.(Trying to hold back anger). How would you like to explain your little joke to the principal? He might think it's so funny he'll invite your parents to hear it!

6. Teenage boy.(Scornfully). Aw, come on. Everybody else is going to try it. Are you chicken?

7. Teenage girl. (Shocked, maybe even frightened). Wow! What did you tell your parents?

8. Teenage boy. (Filled with anger and resentment). You can't tell me what to do! I'm not a little kid anymore!!

Scenes

Just as short stories are written in paragraphs, plays are written in scenes. In each scene, one point or effect is made. The scenes are joined together into acts. Some plays are only one act long; many have three acts.

In each scene, the action builds as more conflicts are created. At the end of a scene, the audience should be anxious to find out what happens next.

Using what you have learned about dialogue, write an opening scene for the first act of a play. Remember to write lines for your characters that show what emotions they feel. Some suggested topics for your scene follow.

1. an argument between a mother and daughter about a party
2. a young man and young woman meeting at a party
3. a student getting caught cheating on an exam by his teacher
4. someone convincing a friend to stay in school
5. someone accusing a friend of having lied about something

The One-Act Play

Using what you have learned about setting, stage direction, and dialogue, write a one-act play. Your scenes may be as long or short as you wish, and you may include as many scenes as you need. The main thing to remember is that a play must show the actions, feelings, and thoughts of the characters through what they say.

SECTION SEVEN:

Exploring Poetry

There are many types of poetry. Some are included here for you to try. As you learn about poetry, you can gain strength in expressing and conveying your feelings.

Sound Pattern

Poems are meant to be read aloud. Thus the sound of words in combination is important. Sounds should be used to emphasize or reinforce the meaning of a poem. They should be chosen to suit the meaning of a poem. But a poem is not simply sound added on to meaning. Ideally, meaning and sound become one in poetry.

Three terms used to describe sound pattern are alliteration, consonance, and assonance.

I. *Alliteration* [uh lit er AY shun]

Alliteration is the repetition of the same initial sound in words which are close together. Remember the tongue twister, "She sells sea shells by the seashore"? Tongue twisters are an extreme form of alliteration. A more sophisticated example follows: "The lost lover, holding limp lilacs, longed for his love." As you can see, alliteration can be used to achieve particular effects.

Write alliterative phrases related to each of the following words. Make your phrases descriptive and original.

1. lake
2. spring
3. car
4. party
5. music
6. rat
7. trip
8. classroom
9. breeze
10. foam

II. *Consonance* [KON suh nentz]

Consonance is similar to alliteration, except that the consonant sounds are repeated in the middle and/or at the end of words near each other, instead of at the beginning. For example, in the phrase "tall silver tail" the "l" sound is repeated. Sometimes, consonance is used with alliteration. The phrase "lively long silver tail" is an example.

Using consonance, write phrases related to each of the following words. This is a difficult exercise.

1. hydrant
2. banana
3. person
4. animal
5. residence
6. avenue
7. school
8. October
9. snowflake
10. record

III. *Assonance* [AS eh nentz]

Assonance is like consonance, except that a *vowel* sound (rather than a consonant sound) is repeated in two or more words near each other. An example of this is "stony" and "holy." What vowel sound is repeated in the phrase "faded sleigh"? Notice it isn't the spelling of the word, but the sound of the word, that counts.

Using assonance, write phrases related to each of the following words:

1. taxi
2. telephone
3. wind
4. ocean
5. clothing
6. picnic
7. winter
8. rain
9. computer
10. television

NOTE: Don't confuse alliteration, consonance, or assonance with rhyme. Rhyme occurs when the endings of two or more words are the same. This includes both vowel and consonant sounds. Some examples of rhyme are cat-bat, faded-graded, anguish-languish.

An Eight-Line Poem

Respond to the following with one word, a few words, or a phrase. Don't number your answers. Write the response to each on a separate line. Except for item three (a color), don't name the thing you are writing about. Just describe it so that someone else can understand your feelings about it.

1. Describe the ugliest animal you can think of. Just write a phrase or two about the particular characteristics you dislike in this animal. Don't name the animal.
2. What do you feel like inside when you are very angry?
3. Describe the color that is most displeasing to you. You may name the color, but add some words which indicate why you don't like it.
4. Describe the odor of a skunk or burning trash.
5. Describe a dump or an overflowing garbage can. Tell how it looks and/or smells.
6. Describe the sound of music that you dislike intensely.
7. Describe the taste or texture of some food you really dislike. You may wish to compare it to something else to indicate your feelings.
8. Describe a riot or some other act of violence. Just write a phrase or two about those elements which stand out in your mind.

Now look at your eight lines. Put the title "Hate" at the top of your paper. Think of these lines as a poem. Add another line as a conclusion, if you wish, Rearrange your words, adding, taking out, or substituting words which will improve your poem. Add or subtract lines as necessary.

Look at the following poem which was created by this method.

Hate
Horned, sharply pointed
Churning, tight, explosive
Livid lime green
A piercing foulness which curdles the nose
Rats, rust, flames, and smoke
Dissonant, discordant screams
Bitter taste of tough leather
Angry mobs hurl stones, bombing, burning, blood, life destroyed.

Haiku

The Japanese write poems in a very simple form. The *haiku* [HI Koo] or hokku is a three-line, unrhymed poem composed of five syllables in the first line, seven in the second, and five in the third.

Haiku is very popular in English, and it is not difficult to write. Here are some examples.

February
The bus breezed by me
splashing mud and icy slush
that stuck to my coat.

Morning
A ray of sunlight
bounced off the sleeping sidewalk
and stung my sore eyes.

Happiness
I dreamt I was rich
and had three cars and a boat
and my own bedroom.

No one would suggest this rather mechanical method as an ideal way to write poetry. The exercise merely shows that writing poetry need not be overwhelming.

Note the alliteration in the poem:

line five—*rats, rust*

line six—*dissonant, discordant*

line eight—*bombing, burning, blood*

Try to use alliteration in your writing. Think also about using harsh sounds when you write about ugliness. Use pleasant sounds when your subject is more pleasant.

some harsh sounds: *b, d, g, k, t*

some pleasant sounds: *l, m, n, r, w*

Read your poetry aloud. The sound of your finished poem adds another dimension to the meaning of the words in the poem.

Notice also that some words have a double meaning. This means they can be interpreted two ways.

The phrase "curdles the nose" is one example in the poem you just read. "Curdle" really applies to milk that is sour. In this poem it suggests that meaning, as well as turning the nose up when something is distasteful.

Another example of double meaning is "burning blood." *Burning* refers to fire. The word also means being angry ¢ "fired up" about something. This is especially emphasized ╿ following the word "burning" with "blood."

Here are two more activities.

1. Look back at the exercises in Section One. Can you prove your responses by creating your own questions those on hate) and answering them? Can you m¿ poem from your responses to any of these exercise clude alliteration and words with double meaning you can.

2. Choose an idea (perhaps taken from Section O make up eight or ten questions relating to it. For how does someone look when he is angry? What ╵ like to do most when you are angry? Where wou to go? Then answer your questions, and make poem from your responses.

A couple of suggestions to help you get started writing your own *haiku* follow.

1. Think of an abstract noun, such as happiness, hate, freedom, etc. Then think of a picture or image that illustrates this idea. Describe the mental picture. Don't worry about syllables at this point.

   After you have written a description—probably one sentence—work these words into three lines with the approximate number of syllables required for each line (5-7-5). Play with the words, choose the most descriptive, and make them fit the required syllabic pattern.

   Maybe you'll need to add a word to one line and take out a word from another line. Changing a word to one of its synonyms may help you get the right number of syllables. Don't be afraid to experiment with new words, or even to invent a word, if necessary.

2. Decide on a subject for your *haiku*. Any subject will do. Then brainstorm the possibilities. List as many phrases as you can that relate to the subject. Try to list phrases which appeal to the reader's senses: sight, sound, smell, touch, and taste. Choose your best phrases and work them into three lines, with the required number of syllables per line (5-7-5).

Tanka

The *tanka* [TAHN Kuh], another Japanese form of poetry, is a longer *haiku*. This five-line poem does not rhyme. The first line has five syllables; the second, seven; the third, five; the fourth, seven; and the fifth, seven.

Here are some examples of *tanka* written by students.

> Home
> Lonely, empty place—
> Broken windows, hanging doors
> Rotted floors, peeled walls
> Roaches and rats playing tag,
> Cries out to the hopeless—home.

> Thunderstorm
> The weirdly colored
> Silent dark oppressive sky
> Threatening to storm
> Softly groans, grumbles, then cracks
> And it gives its flashing grin.

Now try your hand at writing some five-line poems.

Shaped Verse

Shaped verse can perhaps be described as picture poetry. That is, the words are used visually to form a picture which relates to the theme or shows the meaning of the poem. The following is an example of shaped verse.

The Bell

The
Bell Rings
And rings its
Deep peels of joy,
Sorrow, love, and hate
It rings and it echoes, and
It rings once again, 'til the
Privacy of thought, and of mind
That I hold, alone, resounds
Becoming public, becoming lost
To
Me.

Try writing two or three shaped poems. Choose any subject or theme that you wish.

Diamond-Shaped Poetry

Ready to try another poem? This form is a bit more difficult. You can, however, forget rhyme, rhythm, and number of syllables.

If you want to try using the form below, you can write a poem in the shape of a diamond. Read the student examples first.

line 1: Noun
line 2: Two adjectives describing the noun
line 3: Three participles (-ed, -ing)
line 4: Four nouns, or a phrase about the noun
line 5: Three participles that begin to show a change in the subject
line 6: Two adjectives which continue the idea of change
line 7: Noun, the opposite of the subject (the noun in line 1)

Victory
Powerful, highest
Fighting, conquering, striving
Winning is sometimes losing
Pushing, overthrowing, destroying
Down, defeated
Loss.

Morning
Crackling, crisp
Glistening, gleaming, glaring
Sun that stings my eyes
Rushing, raging, tiring
Soothing, sleepy
Evening.

Enemies
Silent, bitter
Fighting, hating, hurting
At last, face to face
Asking, thinking, hoping
Talking, laughing
Friends.

A Five-Line Poem

Here is a suggestion for writing a five-line poem. You don't have to worry about rhyme, rhythm, or syllables.

If you'd like to try it, follow this pattern.

line 1: A noun (also the title of your poem)

line 2: Two adjectives which describe the noun

line 3: Three verbs, used as adjectives, showing what the noun does

line 4: A short phrase about the noun

line 5: A synonym for the noun in line one

Read this five-line poem written by a student. Then try writing one of your own.

> Crackers
> Munchy, tasty
> Salted, crunched, crinkled
> Fun to eat
> Saltines

Free Verse

A poem written in free verse departs from strict rhythm and rhyme. Most poets writing in free verse try to imitate normal speech. This form allows a poet an almost limitless variety of possible effects.

But you still must take care in writing free verse. You need to think about what you are going to write. After you write your first version, you will want to improve it.

Pay particular attention to sound in writing free verse. Read your poetry out loud. Do sound and meaning go together to create one effect?

Below is a student poem. After reading it, write two of your own.

The Darkness
The darkness hides my face, my tears.
The circles in my mind are
   ever-changing, never-ending.
Accept death or fight to live?
A dead-end road appears
And loneliness stalks the sidewalk.
Then the darkness hides my face, my tears,
And me.

NOTE: Student writers of free verse often ask, "How do you know when to begin a new line?" There is no magic formula for knowing. Choose the visual design that you think is best for your poem. Your opinion decides the issue.

Rhymed Verse

Writing a poem in rhyme is easier than you may think. You have read rhymes in books and heard them on television. Now is the time to write your own rhymed verse.

There are many common rhyme schemes. To determine the rhyme scheme of a poem, you assign a letter to each new rhyming sound at the end of the line. The rhyme scheme of this stanza is ABAB:

> So rhymes and schemes are just a task,
> With this I disagree;
> And I'd say proudly, should you ask,
> Mine reads ABAB.

Notice that the last words (the A's) in the first and third lines rhyme. The last words (the B's) in the second and fourth lines rhyme. Another common rhyme scheme is AABB. In this form, the last words of the first two lines rhyme, and the last words of the last two lines rhyme.

Try writing at least eight lines of rhymed verse. You may use any rhyme scheme you wish. What can you create?

The Limerick

A very popular type of rhymed verse is the limerick
[LIM uh rik]. Limericks are fun and challenging to write.
They have both melody and rhythm.

The rules are simple. The first, second, and fifth lines con-
tain no more than nine syllables each. The third and fourth
lines have no more than six syllables.

But you don't have to worry about counting syllables. Once
you have read a limerick aloud, you will feel the rhythmic pattern. You will then be able to duplicate it.

The major goal is to make the reader smile or chuckle.
Perhaps a pun in the last verse will do it. Possibly by twisting
the expected, you will succeed. Read the limerick below and
then write two of your own.

> There once was a fellow named Dirk,
> Whose work was to clerk for a Turk;
> When he said he would quit,
> The old Turk had a fit,
> And was irked by young Dirk's perky smirk.

Learning About Feelings

So far, the exercises on poetry have been rather mechanical. At its best, poetry expresses and conveys feelings. The poem that follows is a character study, but it also has a story to tell. Most importantly, the poem shows the writer's feelings.

About School

He always wanted to say things. But no one understood.
He always wanted to explain things. But no one cared.

Sometimes he would just draw and it wasn't anything.
He wanted to carve it in stone or write it in the sky.
He would just lie out on the grass and look up in the sky
and it would be only him and the sky and the things
that needed saying.

And it was after that, that he drew the picture. It was a
beautiful picture. He kept it under his pillow and
would let no one see it.
And he would look at it every night and think about it.
And when it was dark, and his eyes were closed, he
could still see it.
And it was all of him. And he loved it.

When he started school, he brought it with him. Not to
show anyone, but just to have it with him like a
friend.

It was funny about school.
He sat in a square, brown desk like all the other square,
brown desks and he thought it should be red.
And his room was a square, brown room. Like all the
other rooms. And it was tight and close. And stiff.

He hated to hold the pencil and the chalk, with his arms
stiff and his feet flat on the floor, stiff, with the teacher
watching and watching.
And then he had to write numbers. And they weren't

anything. *They were worse than the letters that could be something if you put them together.*

And the numbers were tight and square and he hated the whole thing.

The teacher came and spoke to him. She told him to wear a tie like all the other boys. He said he didn't like them and she said it didn't matter.

After that they drew. And he drew all yellow and it was the way he felt about morning and it was beautiful.

The teacher came and smiled at him. "What's this?" she asked. "Why don't you draw something like Ken's drawing? Isn't it beautiful?"

It was all questions.

After that his mother bought him a tie and he always drew airplanes and rocket ships like everyone else. And he threw the old picture away.

And when he lay out alone looking at the sky, it was big and blue and all of everything, but he wasn't anymore.

He was square inside and brown, and his hands were stiff, and he was like everyone else. And the thing inside him that needed saying didn't need saying anymore.

It had stopped pushing. It was crushed. Stiff.
Like everything else.

Questions on plot: What is the conflict in the poem? Where is the climax or turning point?

Questions on character: What does the poem show about the boy's character? What kind of person do you think he is? What does the poem tell you about the teacher? Do you know people like the boy or his teacher?

Questions on emotion: What words does the boy use to express his real feelings? What does the poem say about the boy's experience in school? Why was it painful?

Try writing a poem that expresses your own feelings. Include elements of plot and character.

SECTION EIGHT:

Related Activities

Here are some enjoyable creative activities. These are not very formal. They are meant to be fun. Each exercise gives you a chance to express yourself in a new and different way.

Improvisation

Improvisations, or "Improvs," are short plays that are made up by the actors *as* they go along acting out the parts, or roles, the director gives them. All you need for an improv are some willing actors, a cleared area of the classroom, and a beginning idea of the scene.

One person should be the director, plan the improv, tell the actors who they are in the scene and what they are supposed to try to do.

Here is a list that will help you:

1. *Characterization.* Tell each person who he or she is supposed to be. (An old soldier, a pretty young girl, a spy, etc.)

2. *Setting.* Describe the place where the actors meet. (A hotel lobby, the Sahara desert, a restaurant kitchen, etc.) Tell as much as you can so that the actors can imagine themselves in the place described: is it hot or cold or raining, is it attractive as a place, or ugly and rundown, is it day or night, is the time past, present, or future?

3. *Goals.* Tell each actor what he or she is supposed to accomplish or gain from the other characters in the scene. In some cases you may want to tell each actor what his goal is in secret so that the actors only gradually become aware of each other's plans. The improv is usually better when the players' goals are at cross-purposes.

It is important for the director to know when to *stop* the improv. Stop the actors when they seem to have gone as far as they can towards reaching their separate goals and have run out of ways to gain them.

Graffiti

The words or phrases you see all around you are often called graffiti [gra FEET ee]. People, when they aren't being watched, write their names, and sometimes messages, on train station walls, on posters in buses, on bridges, on rocks, and on viaducts. Graffiti can be angry or ugly—four-letter words written by persons who feel the need to express their loneliness, or hatreds or wants. But graffiti can also be very funny, or very clever. They often make true statements about life and society.

During World War II, some American soldier in Europe began to write the message "Kilroy was here" wherever he went. Soon, our troops saw this message everywhere. Kilroy, it seemed, had been to every battle area ahead of them. It helped to cheer up our troops.

Create some graffiti of your own. With your teacher's permission, put butcher paper or newsprint on the bulletin board or a wall in your classroom. Each student can contribute his graffiti, at a time designated by the teacher.

Include sketches and drawings as well as writing. Try using some of the graffiti that either you or your classmates invent as topics for writing.

Posters

Write a phrase or sentence using the images you created in Section One. Make a poster, adding illustrations or designs. The illustrations should act to further clarify your image. If possible, work with a classmate. One person supplies the words; the other, the art work.

What Do You See?

Use the following pictures any way you want to as a source for a poem or a story.

SECTION NINE:

For the Future

Below are listed some tips on writing effectively. They are helpful in all kinds of writing. This is not a list to be memoized. However, you will want to refer to it often.

1. Decide what you're going to write and stick to it. Don't quit when you hit a snag. You can solve the problem. Problems are part of the writing experience.

2. Don't preach. No reader likes to be lectured. Let your story or poem speak for itself.

3. In writing a story or a poem primarily about yourself, make other characters as important as you are.

4. Read your work aloud before stating that it's finished. Things will sound bad to you that don't show up when read silently.

5. Revise. Rewrite. Make a first draft and don't cheat on it. Know that you're going to go over your first draft to improve it. There is no real short-cut to good writing.

6. Be yourself. When you write, write naturally. You can learn a great deal by imitating others, but you should try to find your own voice. Be aware of your own feelings. As an individual you have as much to say as anyone else.

7. Avoid ornamental writing for its own sake. The best language is not always the most flowery language. Why use a fifty-cent word when a ten-center will do? If you use fancy language in a plain situation, you and your reader won't like it.
8. Omit unnecessary words. Don't "pad" your writing. Let others be long-winded. You be clear.
9. Don't take your reader's knowledge for granted. Keep the questions of a reporter in mind: Who? What? When? Where? How? Why? Does the reader know who is speaking? Does he know how your characters got into their situation?
10. Experiment. When you try something new you broaden your skills and your interests.

The Last Word

There is no *one* way to learn creative writing. This book has explored some approaches. There is much more for you to learn. No matter what you write, keep yourself in touch with your feelings. If you honestly express your true feelings, enjoyment and accomplishment are yours.